Dearest Linda

For You

A collection of prayer poems

Wonderful woman in purple!

Much love

by

Ayaz

Ayaz

August 2015.

Grosvenor House
Publishing Limited

This book is published by
Grosvenor House Publishing Ltd
28-30 High Street, Guildford, Surrey, GU1 3EL.
www.grosvenorhousepublishing.co.uk

A CIP record for this book
is available from the British Library

ISBN 978-1-78148-385-5

For You
my beloved Sara

To the best that
I can
I will not bend
And betray You
Following truth
Is like a scent
You have laid
For the bloodhound
Nose
Sometimes leading
Where wild geese
Seem to drop off the edge
Of this flat world
But mostly
A hue and cry
Across open fields
Enjoying the freedom
Of Pure Pursuit
As full expression
Of why You
Unleashed me
In this Way

Just
For You!

Kalwijk
August 2015.

These poems have been largely inspired by the Open Path Sufi Way community of which Angus Landman is a practising member. "Ayaz" is his Sufi name given to him by his Pir, Elias Amidon.

All profits from the sale of this book will be donated to the Sufi Way organisation furthering the development of "awakening and friendship". (www.sufiway.org)

"Practice and all is coming"
K.Patabis Jois

1

I lean into You
Like a child
In to a head wind
Giggling
Sometimes the wind drops
And gasps me with delight
In truth there is nothing
But the wind
Since there is no You
Without me
Giggling.

2

Tethered
Like a boat
On some old sea anchor somewhere
Forced into some shape
Not of my choosing,
I have one glimpse of You
Beloved
And the constraint of form in time
Makes sense.

3

I know You are here
Everywhere I look
Announces Your presence
Every knot of my prayer mat
Is independently joyous
The more I pay attention
And tend emptiness
The more amazed am I
At all this
For which You ask
Nothing in return.

4

I know You are always here
Just close my eyes
And in that eternal moment
The World is rearranged
A lightning fast scene change
There is no space between us
Except in thought
So when I stop thinking
Sunlight pours through
The window
With such enthusiasm
It can't help but shatter the glass.

5

So tender You appear
Between cracks in things
I feel myself ache
And expand
Stretching skin
Like a balloon filling from the inside
Until all of a sudden
It all becomes too much
The balloon bursts
And Emptiness reasserts itself.

6

You are constant
No matter the prevailing wind
Or dust fall on a wrinkled day
The clocks move
And by the hour
The temporal troops forward
Burying what was new once
But not You
You've seen it all before
And watched the cycles
And the wheels turn
Ageless timeless empty constant
Love
You are
Behind the whisper and the roar

And if I could root for You
Somewhere deep
Amid the desperation and despair
And begin to live
As though nothing else mattered
I know you would be revealed to me
Moment to moment
A slowly dawning realisation
Of what has always been
but yet unknown to me
Ageless timeless empty constant
Love
You are behind the whisper and the roar.

7

In every moment I am free
To turn my face towards the sun
And receive Your blessing
The content
The infinite ebb and flow of sand and dust
Does not matter
The constant emptiness of Your regard
Ripens me
And turns my heart
Inside out to reveal the sun
Blazing inside.

8

This is not madness
It is revelation
There is apparently
Not much difference
Except in revelation
The pain of the World becomes mine
And I am to be found
Weeping at the foot of the cross.

9

Everything revealed
Is an access point to You
There is not a dusty corner
In all the world
Where Your bespattered face
And glistening eyes
Do not shine forth
Get your brooms out everybody
And make sure you get right into
The corners.

10

Only You know
The back story to my life
No matter what happens
You remind me the Open Sky
Is only ever a glance upwards
And how blessed am I that I also know
That if ever I get stuck somewhere
And can't move my head
Or my eyes are blinded in confusion
And the raw rimmed saltiness of my tears
That You
You
Will simply move the sky for me.

11

If not for You
For whom do I open my eyes?
Realising a love like this
In due course
Changes the order of things
With each moment
Becoming nothing less
Than a crucifixion
Leaving the Open Sky
Free for birdsong.

12

Resting in You
I am eased
And yet the vital
Remains constant
The call of Your love
And the love of Your calling
Seeping through rock
Overwhelming gratitude.

13

When the Emptiness
In me
Meets the Emptiness in You
Distance has no meaning
Nor does the time
That does condemn
Gratitude becomes a raging torrent
And beauty a wildfire
By which I am in turn
Scorched
And swept away.

14

Suffering is only ever
About the apparent beginning
And end of You
The realisation of Your constancy
The pilgrims progress
The meditative prayer
Soften and dissolve
The edge of what appears to be so
Leaving only
A certain unfathomable
Delighted Being.

15

Finding You
Remembering You
Remembering to remember You
This is The Practice
Not only in the blessed cloister
But in the wilderness
At the beginning of
Every moment
Alone.

16

The walled garden
Needs its walls
To delight

Boundaries
Become sacred
As the context
Becomes clear

You see
Form has no meaning
For me
Except as an ally
In the Glorious Project
To come to know
You.

17

In a moment of tasting
The I that is You
The capsized world
Is righted
Within me

Like an old puzzle finished
I throw myself back in the box
To be revealed again and again
With such delight
And gratitude.

18

I see now
I am preparing to die
into You

Like a morning mist
on soft hills
I feel the contours
Of this suffering land

I soothe and bathe
Where I can
'Til someday
I look skywards
And am gone.

19

You have been wearing me Beloved
And all along I thought I was alone

So thin am I now
Skin is all that separates us
A candle flickering
Both sides of parchment

You have been wearing me Beloved
And all along
I thought I was alone.

20

Slowly
I am beginning to understand
That I cannot see You with my eyes
But only with my heart

For so long I have been
Trying to catch a glimpse of You
Staring madly
Into the middle distance

Now effortlessly
In moments
You are here
My heart empties
Into You
And I am no more.

21

How I approach You
Is of no interest to You
The word sacred has no meaning
Ruined and rusty
I appear
At the garden gate
And the exquisite roses
Sublime in form and perfume
Bow down.

22

I am alive in this
Blessed moment
For the sole purpose
Of feeling the sun
Full upon my face.

23

I carry the Sky for You
It's my only purpose
In so doing
I know what it's like
To become Your Song
To be sung into and out of
No need to compose
Or conduct anymore
What freedom and peace
When I do Your bidding.

24

One taste of You
Reminds me to settle down
With beauty
No matter the apparent
Madness of the World.

25

When I asked You to hold me
I realised You were already carrying me
When I asked You to carry me
I realised
Every cell of me
Was already held
Tender in Your hand
A snowflake
On the very edge
Of existence
On the very edge
Of melting into You.

26

Like a fisherman
Trawling the night sky
Where stars and dreams
Swim in and out
Of each other
I return with my catch
To offer You
I'm a bit better
At casting my net these days
It's true
But in the end
The drift
The wind
The waves the sun and moon
Your hand
Are what fill it
I
I am just a fisherman
Doing my job.

27

I'm sorry
I can't help it
At day break
It's my job
(For the time being at least)
To hang around
At the back door
Kicking dust
And bursting blisters
Feeding on scraps
With the dogs
It's my job
To be on hand
With my empty pages
Ready at any moment
To write down
What you tell me.

28

You listened to the stories
Of the little ones
Rapt
I watched you
Of course I know
You were there all along
In each adventure
intimately shedding tears
Suffering truth together
And here You are
All these years later
Still dying with compassion
Doing and undoing
My shoelaces
Beloved
How wonderous Thou art

29

It's so easy to get lost
In the detail
The scrapes and scraps
Of everyday bloodletting
The angle of the sun
The shape of the clouds
Knowing You
I come to know
My story
From the inside out.

30

You are teaching me
Not to fight
Not to set up in opposition
Teaching me that faith
Is about
Trusting more and more
Deeply
The absolute truth
That Love has no opposite
Not as abstraction
But as melting moment
A trickle
A puddle a flow
Where once there was
But ice.

31

The empty page
Is threatening
To those who need
To work hard
To fill it
But to those
Who lay it
Across the muddy puddle
For You to walk over
What a joy
To have saved
Your feet from getting wet.

32

Last night
I kept switching my lights
On and off

The owls at first
Must have wondered
What was going on
Then they realised
Of course
Being owls
And wise in such matters
Your longing
Is not a respecter
Of time or place
Or person or thing
It is a continual
Announcement
The light going on and off
Is just me being silly
And trying to go to sleep.

33

In the end
There is nothing
Going on here
Only the wind blowing
Down the endlessly
Empty street
I'm beginning to learn
What you're telling me
To save my breath
Shouting at this that
And the other
And let the wind do the work
Emptying that which
Is already empty
Is not my business
Even if it were possible.

34

Faith knows You
Beloved
In the way
The tide knows
The moon
Longing for union
Up and down
The rasping beach
Pulled by the deep
Nowhere.

35

Finding You
Random Grace
Out of which
All birdsong comes
I can bear witness
To let grief echo
And so find its peace
In Your
Effortless Embrace.

36

There is nothing wrong here
How could there be?
There is only the tide
Of You
Coming in and out
Wearing down resistance
Turning all to sand
Until finally the Empty Beach
Blessed be.

37

In a constant succession
Of moments
You remind me
I am
Forgiven
Resurrected
Blessed
The way You scatter light
And play with shadows
The way beauty is suffered
By Your Infinite Expression
Most of the time
I can't see it
But in moments
In random sacred moments
When the curtains are parted
Briefly by the wind
A glimpse
Melts my heart of all resistance
And truth reveals
I am Yours.

38

The field of love
Like gravity
Exerts Your reach and pull
There can be no rank
In Your order
Subjecting stars
Sweet and sour
To equal tenderness
Only a quieting of my resistance
In the faith
This beautiful ground
Will take my weight
When the moment comes.

39

Emptiness
Like a clear current
Keeps washing the muddy
Waters of my effort

Faith knows
That prior to all this
You Are
Clear current
Rising from the deep
Nowhere.

40

Inside the inside
Within the within
You Are
Beloved
And the only way
To reach you
Is to evaporate
Ice, water, steam
And perhaps along
Some distant moment
A beauty passing
In the corridor.

41

In the passing world
She rises
And she sets
In the practice
Each beautiful moment
And moment's beauty
Becomes a
Pillow talk with You
Requiring nothing of me
Whatsoever.

42

Coming into alignment
With You
That is The Practice
Finding the sweet spot
Where the effort
Is all Yours
The sailor finds the wind
The surfer the wave
The poet
The heartbreak
Behind which You
Patiently
Eternally
Are.

43

Coming to know You
Is like being
Dismantled from the inside
One tenacious fibre
At a time
Slowly a space opens
Then a chamber
Then the sky
Into which
Flocks of doves
Are constantly being released.

44

I never thought
I would be on my knees
Before You
Such was the depth
Of my sleep

But such is the power
Of Your mighty spring
The bloom and blossom
Open my heart in gratitude
To the sky
To be fed on
By all who wish to feed
Eternally undiminished.

45

When the knowing comes
I love You
And I seem to know
What that means
In the moment
I am possessed
By an expanding sky
No longer bothered
Which way the birds fly
Or in need of direction
To the four corners
Or even what upside down
Means
Without opposition
I am free
Possessed only
By that expanding sky
And so
When the knowing comes
I seem to know
What loving You
Means.

46

The world was a mystery
Before I met You

Now though
The most complex equations
Seem to end in the flourish
Of an empty sky
And the deepest beauty
In a golden field somewhere
Even the everyday sorrow
That makes me cry
Reminds me to stay
Present to my own crucifixion
And bless You
With all of my might.

47

Somewhere deep
You are the beginning
And end of me

As fire You make
As wind You shape
My destiny

My practice
Is to be easy as smoke
Driven and drifted

In the moments I am
The sky becomes me
In the moments I oppose
The turbulence
However slight
Can be seen
From across the valley.

48

You are the still point
Of all that spins
Yet I don't share You
With anyone
Love like fire
Is indivisible
A billion candles
Can be lit
From one tiny flame
Not only without
Diminishment
But with an eagerness
To set alight
Whatever finds itself
Touched.

49

You bear witness
To my confession
And every beauty
Is Your response
Not as absolution
Nor forgiveness
But as evidence
That love is prior to
And without need
Of anything from me
Whatsoever.

50

To make this work
I have had to put myself
In the way of You
There is nothing of me
Here
Except pencil lines
On white paper
And bruises where
I have resisted
Your insistence.

Lightning Source UK Ltd.
Milton Keynes UK
UKOW04f1816110815

256768UK00001B/1/P